I am an Alligator

Karen Durrie

www.av2books.com

MEDIA ENHANCED BOOKS
AV² BY WEIGL™
ADDED VALUE • AUDIO VISUAL

Go to www.av2books.com, and enter this book's unique code.

BOOK CODE

R417906

AV² by Weigl brings you media enhanced books that support active learning.

AV² provides enriched content that supplements and complements this book. Weigl's AV² books strive to create inspired learning and engage young minds in a total learning experience.

Your AV² Media Enhanced books come alive with...

Audio
Listen to sections of the book read aloud.

Video
Watch informative video clips.

Embedded Weblinks
Gain additional information for research.

Try This!
Complete activities and hands-on experiments.

Key Words
Study vocabulary, and complete a matching word activity.

Quizzes
Test your knowledge.

Slide Show
View images and captions, and prepare a presentation.

... and much, much more!

Published by AV² by Weigl
350 5th Avenue, 59th Floor New York, NY 10118
Website: www.av2books.com www.weigl.com

Library of Congress Cataloging-in-Publication Data

Durrie, Karen.
 I am an alligator / Karen Durrie. -- 1st ed.
    p. cm. -- (I am)
 Includes bibliographical references and index.
 ISBN 978-1-61913-221-4 (hardcover : alk. paper) -- ISBN 978-1-61913-222-1 (softcover : alk. paper)
 1. Alligators--Juvenile literature. I. Title.
 QL666.C925D87 2013
 597.98'4--dc23
                                    2011042511

Printed in the United States of America in North Mankato, Minnesota
1 2 3 4 5 6 7 8 9 0 16 15 14 13 12

012012
WEP060112

Project Coordinator: Karen Durrie Art Director: Terry Paulhus

Weigl acknowledges Getty Images as the primary image supplier for this title.

I am an Alligator

In this book, I will teach you about

- myself
- my food
- my home
- my family

and much more!

I am an alligator.

4

I can stay
as still as a rock.

6

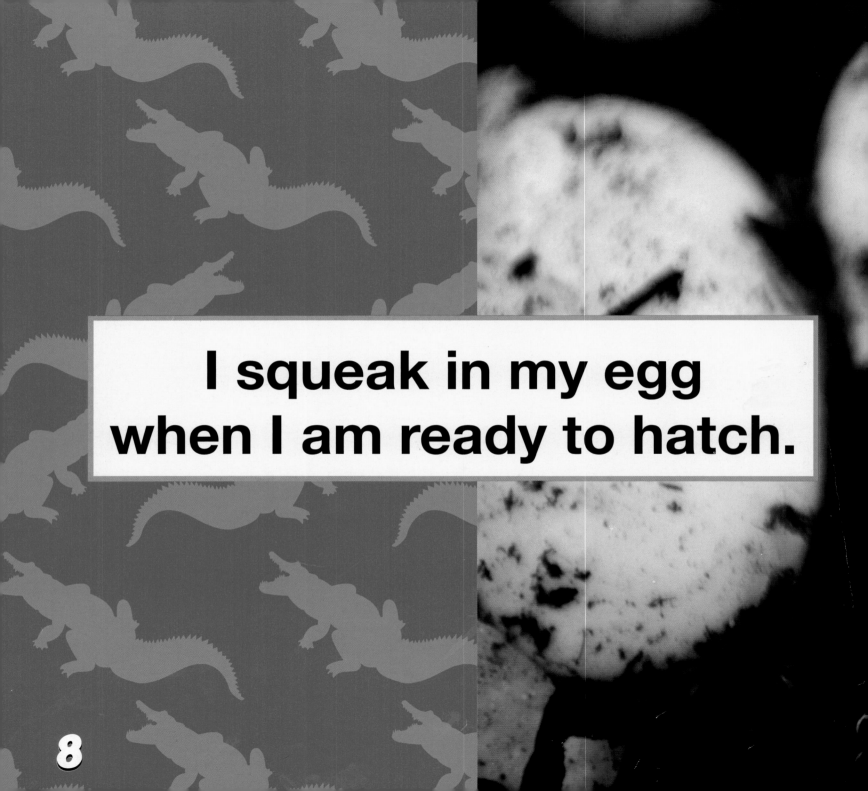

I squeak in my egg when I am ready to hatch.

9

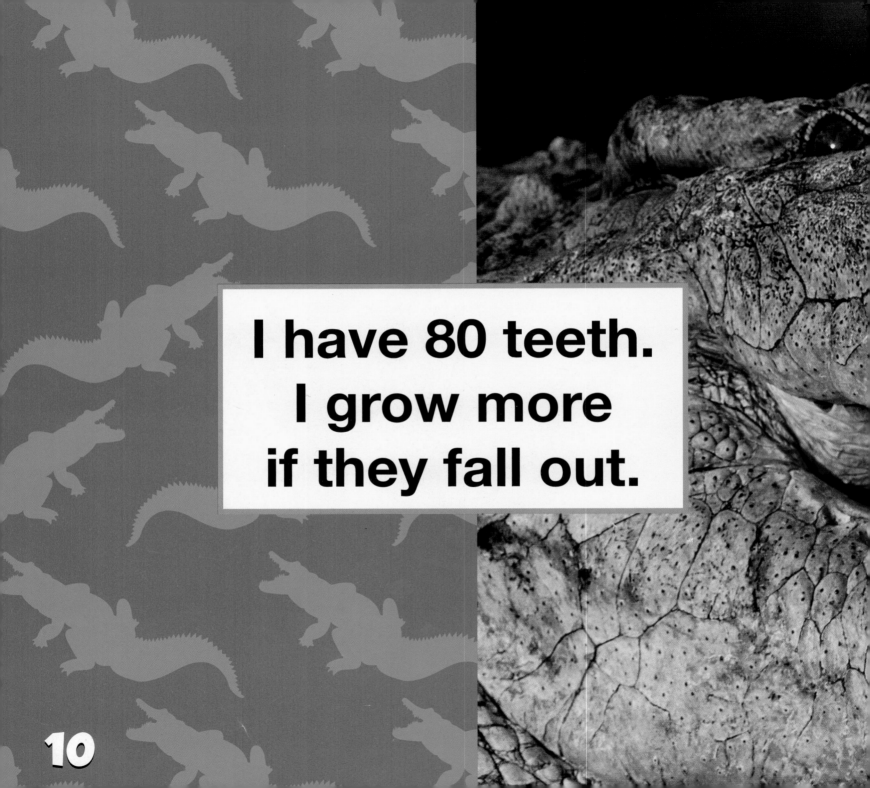

I have 80 teeth.
I grow more
if they fall out.

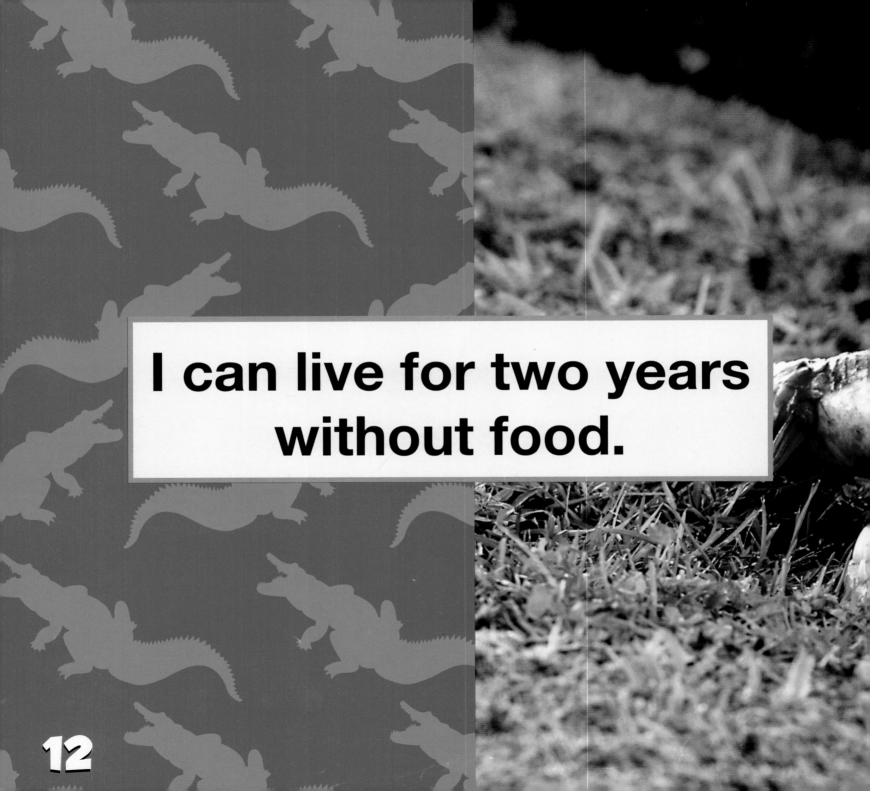

I can live for two years without food.

12

13

I have jaws so strong they can crush bones.

14

I have lived on Earth for millions of years.

I need the Sun to get warm.

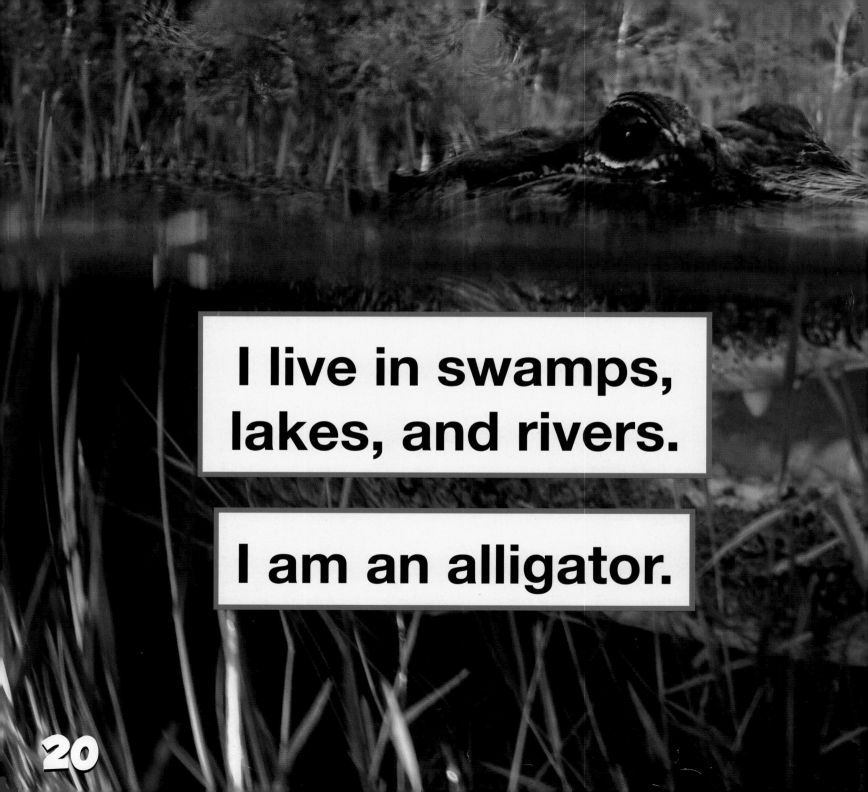

I live in swamps, lakes, and rivers.

I am an alligator.

21

ALLIGATOR FACTS

These pages provide detailed information that expands on the interesting facts found in the book. They are intended to be used by adults as a learning support to help young readers round out their knowledge of each amazing animal featured in the I Am series.

Pages 4–5

I am an alligator. Alligators are the largest reptile in North America. They have bony plates covered in leathery skin, which makes them appear spiky. They can weigh up to 1,000 pounds (454 kg) and can reach more than 13 feet (4 meters) in length.

Pages 6–7

Alligators can stay as still as a rock. Alligators stand or float motionless in the water with just their nostrils and eyes showing. They can be still for hours. This allows the alligator to surprise prey that comes close enough to be caught.

Pages 8–9

Alligators squeak in their eggs when they are ready to hatch. Alligator mothers make nests on land to lay eggs in. They then guard the eggs until they hatch. Baby alligators squeak when they are ready to hatch, and the mother helps break them out of their eggs. She then carries her babies in her mouth to the water.

Pages 10–11

Alligators have 80 teeth and grow more if they fall out. An alligator grows as many as 3,000 teeth in its lifetime. Teeth are one way to tell alligators and crocodiles apart, since they look similar. An alligator's teeth do not show when its mouth is closed. In a crocodile, the fourth tooth shows outside its jaw.

Alligators can live for up to two years without food.
Alligators eat fish, frogs, birds, and other animals. An alligator can eat the equivalent of 500 hamburgers in one meal. Alligators can go long periods between feedings because they do not use food to help warm their bodies. Fat stores give them energy.

Alligators have jaws so strong they can crush bones.
Their jaws and teeth can grip and crush prey with ease. Alligators have the strongest bite force of any animal. Their bite produces as much force as a car falling on top of a person.

Alligators have lived on Earth for millions of years.
Alligators are members of the crocodile family, which scientists say have lived on Earth for more than 200 million years. They lived at the same time as dinosaurs, and fossils show that their bodies are still the same today.

Alligators need the Sun to get warm. Alligators are cold blooded. This means they cannot produce their own body heat. Their body temperature comes from the environment around them. Alligators bask in the Sun if they are cool, and they find shade or water when they are hot.

Alligators live in swamps, lakes, and rivers. Alligators were once endangered. Laws made to protect them have raised their numbers to more than one million in Florida, Louisiana, Texas, and Georgia. Their main threats today are loss of freshwater habitat, pollution, and hunters.

WORD LIST

Research has shown that as much as 65 percent of all written material published in English is made up of 300 words. These 300 words cannot be taught using pictures or learned by sounding them out. They must be recognized by sight. This book contains 33 common sight words to help young readers improve their reading fluency and comprehension. This book also teaches young readers several important content words, such as nouns. These words are paired with pictures to aid in learning and improve understanding.

Page	Sight Words First Appearance	Page	Content Words First Appearance
4	am, an, I	4	alligator
6	a, as, can, still	6	rock
8	in, my, to, when	8	egg
10	grow, have, if, more, out, they	10	teeth
12	food, for, live, two, without, years	14	bones, jaws
14	so	16	millions
16	Earth, lived, of, on	18	Sun
18	get, need, the	20	lakes, swamps
20	and, rivers		

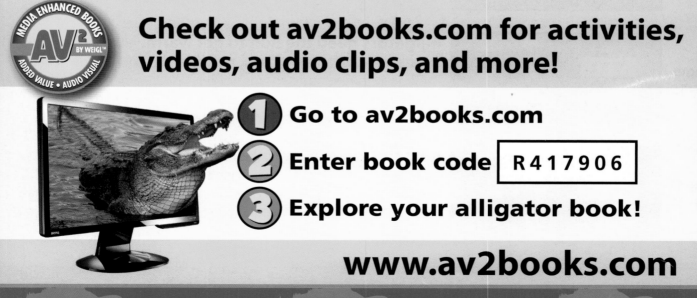